The Evidence of
Things Not Seen

T0035539

HE FIRE NEXT TIME

ANOTHER COUNTRY

JIMMY'S
RHYTHM & BLUES

THE EXTRAORDINARY LIFE OF JAMES BALDWIN

Written by
Michelle Meadows

Illustrated by
Jamiel Law

HARPER
An Imprint of HarperCollins Publishers

Home is brick brown,
Harlem, uptown,
trains rumbling by.

Born and raised in the heart of Harlem,
James Baldwin grew up
playing on the rooftop,
living in books,
dreaming about changing the world.

Friends and family called him Jimmy.

Jimmy lived in a cramped apartment,
where he took care of his little brothers and sisters.

In between changing diapers and giving baths,
Jimmy flipped through the pages of books.

He read everything and everywhere,
often holding a baby and a book
at the same time.

David Baldwin Sr. didn't like Jimmy reading
books other than the Bible.
His father was a preacher
and a harsh, rigid man.

Jimmy's mother was quite the opposite.
Berdis smiled at Jimmy, protected him,
and showed him love.

Outside is cement gray,
hard, cold concrete
crumbling, cracking . . .

Along with preaching on Sundays,
Jimmy's father worked at a soda factory during the week.
Jimmy's mother cleaned houses.

David and Berdis did the best they could,
but like many families during the Great Depression,
they struggled to feed the children.

Sometimes Jimmy led his little brothers on a hunt
for old, cheap bread to eat.

In those same streets,
Jimmy felt the sting of violence and racism
early in life.

When he was ten,
two white police officers searched him in an empty lot
and left him on the ground.

Whether he felt frightened, lonely, sad, or worried,
Jimmy let his emotions pour from his pen.

He wrote everything and everywhere
with his left hand,
sometimes scribbling on paper bags.

Words soothed him.

And whenever he could,
Jimmy slipped away to his favorite hill in Central Park,
where he escaped, wondered, and
imagined the future.

Writing is electric blue,
bright, brilliant swirls
of letters and words
flying, flipping,
flowing to the beat.

In elementary school, Jimmy stood out.
Kids picked on him,
noticing he was small, shy, and smart.

His teachers noticed something else:
Jimmy had a gift for weaving words together
like musical notes of a song.

He wrote songs, poems, plays, and stories.
Writing gave him a voice.

When he wasn't in school, Jimmy devoured books
in the 135th Street library—home of the personal
collection of Arturo Alfonso Schomburg,
a Puerto Rican–born Black historian.

A theater teacher named Orilla Winfield
nurtured Jimmy's talent. Her nickname was Bill.

When Jimmy wrote a school play, Bill directed it.

Bill also took Jimmy to museums, movies,
and plays outside of school.

Berdis was pleased with Bill's support and Jimmy's interest in the arts.

One day, Jimmy shared his deepest dream with his mother:
"I'm going to be a great writer when I grow up."

In junior high school,
Countee Cullen and Herman Porter saw Jimmy's talent too.
Both men lifted him up.

Countee, a prize-winning poet, was a French teacher.
He told Jimmy about his trips to France.
In Countee's literary club,
Jimmy learned poetic form
and spun imaginary tales.

Herman named Jimmy editor of the school magazine.
He took Jimmy downtown to the library on 42nd Street to
do research for an essay tracing Harlem's history.

When people said Jimmy didn't belong downtown because
of his skin color, Herman showed Jimmy he had a right to
be there.

Church is glimmering gold,
  gospel songs, stomping feet,
    tambourines tapping.

As Jimmy grew older, he became scared of many things.

He was scared of his father because of his bad temper.
He was scared of the streets because crime lurked on the stoops.
He was scared of his sexuality because he loved a boy.

Jimmy hoped church would shield him from his fears.

Soaking in the rhythm of gospel music
and the language of the Bible,
Jimmy became a preacher,
a star in the pulpit at age fourteen.

He liked having an audience.
Preaching made Jimmy feel in control of his life.
At least for a while.

When he wasn't preaching, Jimmy took the train from Harlem to DeWitt Clinton High School in the Bronx.

Working on the school's magazine,
Jimmy wrote about topics that weighed heavily on his heart and mind—race, religion, identity, and family.

And he read.

He read books by Russian novelist Fyodor Dostoevsky,
American British novelist Henry James,
and French novelist Honoré de Balzac.

He read about France and dreamed of going there one day.

Jazz is passion purple,
paintbrushes, bebop, blues,
singing, swinging, soul.

On the advice of a friend, Jimmy met a painter.

Knocking on Beauford Delaney's door in Greenwich Village
changed Jimmy's life.

Beauford was kind.
He introduced Jimmy to jazz and the blues,
to the stories of Black people tucked inside music,
to art, color, and light.
He showed Jimmy how to see with an artist's eyes.

Beauford became like a father.
And once the two found each other,
they never let go.

A year later, Jimmy decided he wanted to write
more than he wanted to preach.

This meant letting go of what his father wanted
and facing his fears.

One Sunday, Jimmy preached his last sermon
and tiptoed out of the church.

Over the years, Jimmy also thought of becoming
a musician, a painter, or an actor.

But he saw writing as his special gift—a calling to capture
the voice of his ancestors, stand up for oppressed people,
and push the world to change.

For Jimmy, writing was an act of love and discovery.

Writing helped him discover true power:
the power of his mind,
the power of his words,
and the power of his stories.

And with this power, Jimmy felt unstoppable.

With Beauford's help, Jimmy moved to Greenwich Village.

While waiting tables, he met other creative souls
and became known as a charming, lively storyteller.

He talked and laughed with friends at the restaurant
late into the evening.

At home, Jimmy wrote through the night.
He liked to write longhand on paper with no lines.
Then he typed up passages as he went along.

Writing book reviews and essays helped pay the bills.

Writing a novel about a son, his father, and the church
helped Jimmy explore and understand his life.

He wrote about what he knew and felt in his heart.

A young woman connected Jimmy with Richard Wright,
a famous author who lived in Brooklyn.

Richard read about sixty of Jimmy's pages.
Then Richard and his editor, Edward Aswell,
at Harper & Brothers helped Jimmy get funds
to work on his novel—a five-hundred-dollar grant.

The publisher, Frank MacGregor, even took Jimmy
out to lunch to celebrate.

But Jimmy's initial hopes vanished
when the publisher eventually turned the book down.
Jimmy sank into a pit of despair, wondering
if he would ever realize his big dream.

Paris is fog gray,
    unknown possibilities,
new beginnings, airplane roaring.

By 1948, Jimmy had suffered setbacks,
heartbreaks, the blues,
including the death of close friends and his father.

Jimmy was determined to survive and find his rhythm.
And he knew he couldn't do it in America.

At age twenty-four, he packed his bags
and headed to Paris, France.

When Jimmy arrived in Paris,
he found the freedom to discover who he wanted to be.

Paris was not without hardship.
But for the first time,
Jimmy felt relief from the relentless discrimination in America.

With only a little more than a pen and a notebook,
he wrote in hotels and the Café de Flore.

In Paris, Jimmy fell in love with Lucien Happersberger,
a painter from Switzerland.

On a trip to a Swiss village,
while Lucien painted,
Jimmy tapped away at the keys on his typewriter
with the beat of blues and jazz music in the air.

He listened to the records of Bessie Smith and Fats Waller.
Sometimes he read pages of his book aloud
to Lucien.

The main character, John Grimes, is a poor fourteen-year-old boy
from Harlem who becomes a preacher
and has a strict father.

John looks out over his favorite hill in Central Park and dreams,
just as Jimmy had done in his childhood.

Jimmy had been working on the novel off and on for a decade.

In Switzerland, he finished writing the book in three months.

With Lucien by his side, Jimmy mailed the book to New York.

Go Tell It on the Mountain was published soon after, in May 1953.

Jimmy dedicated the book to his mother and father.

Rage is fire red,
  burning, boiling, blazing,
    heat rising up.

Jimmy went on to publish many more books,
and no matter where he lived,
he always cared deeply
about the struggles of Black people back home.

One day, he saw a photo of a teenager named
Dorothy Counts in the newspaper.
An angry crowd harassed her as she made her way
to school on September 4, 1957.
The hatred and racism shocked Jimmy,
inspiring him as he began a tour of the Southern states.

Jimmy interviewed Southerners,
observing the devastation of white supremacy,
oppression, discrimination, abuse,
and segregation.

His mission was to bear witness to the truth.
He marched, protested,
and brought people together to raise awareness
about justice and equality.

He became a leading voice of the civil rights movement,
writing and speaking eloquently about the fight for freedom

When Jimmy's essay collection *The Fire Next Time*
was released in 1963,
the book deepened the nation's understanding
of the Black experience in America,
delivering urgent warnings
about the dangers of racism.

Jimmy captured the nation's suffering—
the hopes and dreams
for love and humanity—
energizing people of all ages and races
to open their minds to new ways of thinking.

Home is stone silver,
   South of France,
peaceful, healing, welcoming,
      rocking to the rhythm of the sea.

But after the assassinations of Malcolm X, Medgar Evers,
and Dr. Martin Luther King Jr.,
Jimmy was devastated.

In 1971, he moved to a house
in the village of Saint-Paul de Vence.

Overlooking the valley and the Mediterranean Sea,
his house became a place of refuge.

Friends and family gathered around his warm "Welcome Table"
in celebration of joy, love, and inclusion for all people.

From the streets of Harlem
to his travels all around the world,
Jimmy shared his rhythm and blues;
with compassion in his heart and a pen in his hand,
James Baldwin touched lives and changed the world.

AUTHOR'S NOTE

When my editor asked me if I would be interested in writing a picture book about James Baldwin, I immediately got excited about the opportunity to learn more about one of America's greatest writers and intellectuals. I remember reading *Notes of a Native Son* in college and have long admired the sophistication and beauty of James Baldwin's writing style.

James Baldwin authored more than twenty works of fiction and nonfiction, including essays, plays, short stories, poems, and novels.

Sometimes he wandered to different cities or countries, looking for the peace and space to write. He called himself a "transatlantic commuter"—going back and forth between America and Europe. His life in Paris prepared him to go to the South during the civil rights movement. He didn't consider himself a spokesperson for civil rights, yet he became a powerful voice for the movement.

Although he is well known for his writing, James Baldwin appreciated many types of artistic expression. He loved to sing and dance, and he wrote songs in childhood; music was an important part of his life. James Baldwin was also interested in art, such as the colors of clothing, nature, or paintings. Hence the choice to tell his life story through the lens of a variety of colors and with a rhythm that represents the musical flow of his life.

While writing this book, it moved me most to learn how James Baldwin found comfort in words from a young age. Words have always soothed me too. My mother says that when I was a child, I left little notes all around the house about how I was feeling. I hope this book inspires young readers to find joy and power through written expression.

JAMES BALDWIN'S OEUVRE

Go Tell It on the Mountain (1953) · *The Amen Corner: A Drama in Three Acts* (1954) · *Notes of a Native Son* (1955) · *Giovanni's Room* (1956) · *Sonny's Blues* (1957) · *Blues for Mister Charlie: A Play* (1961) · *Nobody Knows My Name: More Notes of a Native Son* (1961) · *Another Country* (1962) · *The Fire Next Time* (1963) · *Nothing Personal* (1964) · *Going to Meet the Man* (1965) · *Jimmy's Blues and Other Poems* (1968) · *Tell Me How Long the Train's Been Gone* (1968) · *One Day When I Was Lost: A Scenario Based on Alex Haley's The Autobiography of Malcolm X* (1969) · *A Rap on Race* (1971) · *No Name in the Street* (1972) · *A Dialogue* (1973) · *If Beale Street Could Talk* (1973) · *Little Man, Little Man: A Story of Childhood* (1976) · *The Devil Finds Work* (1976) · *Just Above My Head* (1979) · *The Evidence of Things Not Seen* (1985) · *The Price of the Ticket: Collected Nonfiction, 1948–1985* (1985) · *Collected Essays* (1998) · *Early Novels and Stories* (1998) · *Fifty Famous People* (2003) · *Native Sons* (2004) · *Vintage Baldwin* (2004) · *The Cross of Redemption: Uncollected Writings* (2011)

TIMELINE

1924: James Arthur Baldwin is born on August 2 in Harlem Hospital in New York. His mother was Emma Berdis Jones and stepfather was David Baldwin Sr. James was the oldest of nine children and became an uncle to a host of beloved nieces and nephews.

1929–41: The Great Depression

1929: Begins elementary school at Public School 24

1937: Writes "Harlem Then and Now" essay for the Frederick Douglass Junior High School magazine, *The Douglass Pilot*

1938: Graduates from Frederick Douglass Junior High School and begins preaching at Fireside Pentecostal Assembly, which he does for about three years

1940: High school friend Emile Capouya connects James with painter Beauford Delaney.

1942: Graduates from DeWitt Clinton High School

1944: Meets writer Richard Wright

1946: James's best friend, Eugene Worth, commits suicide.

1948: Possibly inspired by Richard Wright's move, James leaves New York for Paris, France.

1949: Wrongfully arrested in Paris. James meets Lucien Happersberger in Paris.

1951–52: James and Lucien go to Lucien's family's Swiss chateau, where James finishes his first novel, *Go Tell It on the Mountain*.

1953: *Go Tell It on the Mountain* is published.

1954: Wins a Guggenheim Fellowship

1956: Wins the National Institute of Arts and Letters Award for literature

1957: Returns to the United States after seeing a photograph of Dorothy Counts in a newspaper. He travels throughout the South and interviews protestors; meets Dr. Martin Luther King Jr.

1960: Covers sit-ins in Tallahassee, Florida

1961–70: Lives in Turkey off and on

1963: Wins the Polk Memorial Award for outstanding magazine journalism

1963: Attends March on Washington for Jobs and Freedom

1963: Featured on the cover of *Time* magazine

1963: Medgar Evers is assassinated.

1963: James, Lorraine Hansberry, and others meet with Attorney General Robert F. Kennedy to fight for increased government action on civil rights.

1965: Malcolm X is assassinated.

1968: Dr. Martin Luther King Jr. is assassinated.

1971: James moves to the village of Saint-Paul de Vence in the South of France, where he lives for the last sixteen years of his life.

1978: Receives the Martin Luther King Jr. Memorial Medal

1986: Named Commander of the French Legion of Honor

1987: Dies at age sixty-three from esophageal and stomach cancer on November 30, reported December 1.

2016: The documentary *I Am Not Your Negro*, directed by Raoul Peck, is released.

SELECTED SOURCES

Campbell, James. *Talking at the Gates: A Life of James Baldwin.* Oakland: University of California Press, 1991.

Eckman, Fern Marja. *The Furious Passage of James Baldwin.* Lanham, MD: M. Evans, 1966.

Elgrably, Jordan. "James Baldwin, the Art of Fiction, No. 78," *The Paris Review*, Spring 1984. www.theparisreview.org/interviews/2994/the-art-of-fiction-no-78-james-baldwin.

Leeming, David. *James Baldwin: A Biography.* New York: Knopf, 1994.

National Museum of African American History & Culture. "Chez Baldwin: An Exploration of James Baldwin's Life and Works Through the Powerful Lens of His House 'Chez Baldwin' in St. Paul de Vence, France," *Smithsonian.* www.nmaahc.si.edu/explore/exhibitions/chez-baldwin.

———. "James Baldwin Literary Achievements," *Smithsonian.* www.nmaahc.si.edu/explore/exhibitions/chez-baldwin/literary-achievements.

Pavlić, Ed. *Who Can Afford to Improvise? James Baldwin and Black Music, the Lyric and the Listeners.* New York: Fordham University Press, 2016.

PHOTO CREDITS

An interview at the Whitehall Hotel, photo by Jenkins/Stringer/Hulton Archive via Getty Images.

Presenting a new book in Amsterdam, photos by Rob Croes/Anefo, courtesy of the National Archives.

In Hyde Park, London, photos by Allan Warren. Licensed under CC BY-SA 3.0, available at www.creativecommons.org/licenses/by-sa/3.0.

Giving a lecture, photo by Sjakkelien Vollebregt/Anefo, courtesy of the National Archives.

Getting comfortable to write. Bettmann/Bettman via Getty Images.

Portrait. Library of Congress, Prints & Photographs Division, Carl Van Vechten Collection, LC-DIG-van-5a51683.

In Paris, photo by Sophie Bassouls/Sygma via Getty Images.

For my father, Mel Mitchell, with love and gratitude.
Thank you for teaching me about jazz, art, and Black history.
—M.M.

To my wife and daughter,
Jenny and Aila, for your love, patience, and support.
Thank you for keeping me grounded.
—J.L.

If Beale Street Could Talk

JIMMY'S BLUES AND OTHER POEMS